YOUR PASSPORT TO
SRI LANKA

=18 OCT 2019=

by Nancy Dickmann

CONTENT CONSULTANT

Daniel Bass
Manager, South Asia Program
Mario Einaudi Center for International Studies
Cornell University

CAPSTONE PRESS
a capstone imprint

Capstone Captivate is published by Capstone Press, an imprint of Capstone.
1710 Roe Crest Drive
North Mankato, Minnesota 56003
www.capstonepub.com

Library of Congress Cataloging-in-Publication Data is available on the Library of Congress website.
ISBN: 978-1-4966-9554-3 (hardcover)
ISBN: 978-1-4966-9722-6 (paperback)
ISBN: 978-1-9771-5546-7 (eBook PDF)

Summary:
What would it be like to live in Sri Lanka? How is Sri Lankan culture unique? Explore the sights, traditions, and daily lives of people in Sri Lanka.

Image Credits
Capstone: Eric Gohl, 5; Dreamstime: Mitchell Gunn, 28; iStockphoto: hadynyah, 19; Newscom: REUTERS/Dinuka Liyanawatte, 25; Shutterstock: Aleksandar Todorovic, 11, DESIGNFACTS, 24, Epic_Sam, 14, givaga, cover, Guy Mace Photography, 23, Marius Dobilas, 7, piotreknik, 9, Rawpixel.com, 20, SamanWeeratunga, 27, SJ Travel Photo and Video, 13, Thomas Wyness, 17

Design Elements
iStockphoto: Yevhenii Dubinko; Shutterstock: 10topvector, Flipser, MicroOne, N.Vector Design, pingebat

Editorial Credits
Editor: Clare Lewis; Designer: Juliette Peters;
Media Research: Tracy Cummins; Premedia: Laura Manthe

CONTENTS

Words in **bold** are in the glossary.

CHAPTER ONE

WELCOME TO SRI LANKA!

The sun shines down on a beautiful beach. Clear turquoise water laps at the sand. Palm trees sway in the breeze. The water is full of surfers and swimmers. This is one of Sri Lanka's famous beaches. People come from all over the world to enjoy the sun and sand. But there is much more to this amazing country!

Sri Lanka is an island nation. The island is shaped like a teardrop. It lies in the Indian Ocean, just off the coast of India. Sri Lanka is about the same size as West Virginia. Nearly 23 million people live there. Sri Lanka has close links to India. But it has a culture and identity all its own.

MAP OF SRI LANKA

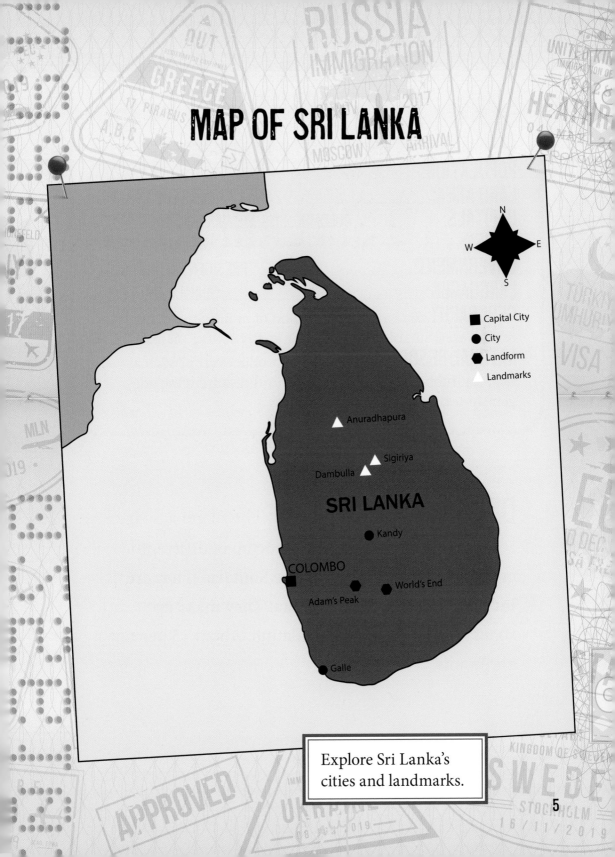

N
W   E
S

■ Capital City
● City
⬡ Landform
▲ Landmarks

▲ Anuradhapura

▲ Sigiriya
Dambulla ▲

SRI LANKA

● Kandy

COLOMBO ■

⬡ Adam's Peak   ⬡ World's End

● Galle

Explore Sri Lanka's
cities and landmarks.

FACT FILE

OFFICIAL NAME: DEMOCRATIC SOCIALIST REPUBLIC OF SRI LANKA
POPULATION: 22,889,201
LAND AREA: 24,954 SQ. MI. (64,630 SQ KM)
CAPITALS: COLOMBO, SRI JAYEWARDENEPURA KOTTE
MONEY: SRI LANKAN RUPEE
GOVERNMENT: PRESIDENTIAL REPUBLIC
LANGUAGES: SINHALA AND TAMIL
GEOGRAPHY: Sri Lanka has a region of mountains in the central area, surrounded by flat or gently rolling plains.
NATURAL RESOURCES: Sri Lanka produces crops such as rice, tea, rubber, and coconuts. Natural resources include gemstones, graphite, and limestone.

DIFFERENT CULTURES

Sri Lanka's population is made up of different groups. The largest group is the Sinhalas. They are **indigenous** people of Sri Lanka. They make up about 75 percent of the population. About 15 percent are Tamils.

Sri Lanka's warm climate, delicious food, and beautiful beaches make it popular with tourists.

Some groups of Tamils have lived in Sri Lanka for centuries. Others first came there from India between the 1840s and 1930s. About 9 percent of Sri Lankans are Muslims. They came to the island centuries ago.

The different groups tend to live in separate areas. They often follow different religions. They speak their own languages and have their own traditions.

CHAPTER TWO

HISTORY OF SRI LANKA

OLD AND NEW

About 2,500 years ago, people began to arrive in Sri Lanka. They came from northern India. They set up Sri Lanka's first kingdom. It was centered around the city of Anuradhapura. People built **temples** and palaces. They also built systems to water crops.

THE FIRST SINHALAS

Sri Lankans tell a story about a prince called Vijaya. Vijaya's father banished him from India, so he and 700 others sailed to Sri Lanka. Legend says that he was the first person to arrive from India. Vijaya defeated the evil spirits who lived there and set up a peaceful kingdom.

BUDDHISM

In about 250 BCE, a new religion arrived. Buddhists from India visited Sri Lanka. They followed the teachings of the Buddha. He was a spiritual leader who founded the Buddhist religion. These people taught others about their religion. Many people soon started to follow **Buddhism**.

SHIPS AND TRADE

Sri Lanka was located on many trade routes. Sailors from Greece and Rome sometimes stopped there. So did ships from Arabia and China. People traded goods and shared ideas. In the 1500s, ships began arriving from Europe as well.

EUROPEANS ARRIVE

Fast ships arrived in Sri Lanka in 1505. They came from Portugal. The Portuguese began to trade in the region. Soon they built a fort. They took control of more of Sri Lanka. They traded cinnamon and elephants with other countries.

FACT

Historical records show that until the 1400s, you could walk from India to Sri Lanka. A path of limestone lies between the two. Most of it is now underwater.

TIMELINE OF SRI LANKAN HISTORY

ABOUT 380 BCE: The first Sinhala capital is founded in Anuradhapura.

ABOUT 250 BCE: The religion of Buddhism arrives in Sri Lanka.

1017: The capital of Sri Lanka moves to Polonnaruwa.

1505: Portuguese traders arrive in Sri Lanka and soon take over.

1658: The Dutch force the Portuguese out of Sri Lanka.

1796: The British take over Sri Lanka and name it Ceylon.

1948: Ceylon becomes an independent country.

1972: The country changes its name from Ceylon to Sri Lanka.

1983: A civil war between the Sinhala-led government of Sri Lanka and Tamil groups begins.

2009: The civil war ends with a government victory.

Some buildings from the British period are in the style of the United Kingdom.

By 1658 the Dutch had forced the Portuguese out. The Dutch ruled Sri Lanka for more than a century. Then, in 1796, the British took over. They named the country Ceylon.

INDEPENDENCE AND WAR

By the 20th century, Sri Lankans wanted to govern themselves. They finally became **independent** in 1948. But not everyone was happy. The Tamils wanted to be separate. A **civil war** began in 1983. It lasted until 2009.

CHAPTER THREE

EXPLORE SRI LANKA

For a fairly small island, Sri Lanka packs a lot in. The beautiful mountains are covered in trees and greenery. The tallest is known as Sri Pada, or Adam's Peak. The region has deep valleys and steep cliffs. One cliff is known as World's End. It is about 4,000 feet (1,220 meters) high!

The rest of Sri Lanka's land slopes gradually down to the sea. There are hot and humid **rain forests**. There are also **grasslands** and farms. Sri Lanka has a rainy season each year. It is called the monsoon.

FACT

The top of Sri Pada mountain is flat. There is a hollow in the rock that looks like a footprint. "Sri Pada" means "holy footprint." Buddhists believe that it was made by the Buddha. Muslims and Christians believe it was made by Adam, the first man in the Bible.

By law, elephants are protected from hunters in Sri Lanka.

AMAZING ANIMALS

Many people visit Sri Lanka to see wildlife. There are large herds of elephants. Leopards slink through the forests. Brightly colored birds fill the trees. Off the coast, there are whales and dolphins.

Sri Lanka has many bell-shaped structures called stupas. They are holy sites for Buddhists.

ANCIENT SITES

Sri Lanka has many historic sites. One of the most famous is Anuradhapura. This city was built thousands of years ago. It was abandoned around 1000 CE. Then it was covered over by jungle. Some of its buildings are still standing. There are temples and pools. Buddhist ceremonies are still held here.

Dambulla is another Buddhist site. It is made up of five caves. Long ago, people built temples in the caves. There are many statues of the Buddha. There are beautiful paintings on the walls.

BUDDHISM IN SRI LANKA

Buddhists follow the teachings of a man known as the Buddha. Buddhists believe that, long ago, he sat under a fig tree to think. He wanted to find answers about life. There is a very old tree in Anuradhapura. It is said to have grown from a cutting of the Buddha's fig tree. It is a holy site for Buddhists.

THE LION ROCK

Sigiriya is in central Sri Lanka. A huge, steep rock towers over the plains. At the top is a **fortress**. A king built it in the late 400s. A huge stone lion once guarded the path to it. Only its feet remain now. Visitors must pass between them to climb to the top.

EXCITING CITIES

Colombo is Sri Lanka's largest city. It is on the island's southwest coast. Ships from many lands once docked in its **harbor**. It is still an important port today. Tourists walk along the city's shady avenues. Many of the buildings date from the time of British rule.

Galle is on the southern coast. The Portuguese used it as their main trading port. The Dutch later built a fort there. The city has many historic buildings. Tourists visit restaurants to try fresh seafood. There are markets, shops, and food stalls.

KANDY

Kandy lies in the forested hills at the heart of the island. It was once the capital of its own kingdom. It still has a vibrant and unique culture. Tourists come to watch colorful parades and festivals. Its name comes from *kanda*, the Sinhala word for *hill*.

In Kandy, drummers play as people perform traditional dances.

CHAPTER FOUR

DAILY LIFE

In Sri Lanka, fewer than 20 percent of people live in cities. The rest live in the countryside. In the cities, many people get around in tuk-tuks. These three-wheeled vehicles are often brightly painted. They are used as taxis. People also sell food from them and make deliveries. Trains connect the island's cities and towns.

EDUCATION

Education is very important in Sri Lanka. About 92 percent of Sri Lankans are able to read. School is free, and most children attend. The school day often starts early. The youngest children only have a few hours of school each day. Older children stay for longer periods.

Most Sri Lankan children wear school uniforms.

Tea is often planted on hillsides so the soil doesn't get too soggy.

GROWING TEA

Many people in the central highlands work on large tea farms. In Sri Lanka, tea leaves are usually picked by hand. This is very hard work. Pickers often work long hours for little pay. Many tea workers live on the plantations. Their families live with them.

RELIGION

Religion plays a large role in Sri Lankan life. About 70 percent of the population is Buddhist. This includes most of the Sinhala people. Many young men and women become Buddhist monks or nuns.

The Tamils are mainly Hindu. There are also many Muslims and Christians. However, in Sri Lanka, the faiths sometimes mix. Some Buddhist temples have statues of Hindu gods. People of all faiths take part in each other's festivals.

LANGUAGES OF SRI LANKA

Sri Lanka has two official languages: Sinhala and Tamil. They are written using different systems. About 75 percent of the population speaks Sinhala. Most of the rest speak Tamil. A few people still speak a language based on Portuguese. It was once used across the country. About 25 percent of the population speaks English as a foreign language.

CURRY

Traders from many lands visited Sri Lanka in the past. They all had an influence on its food. It now reflects a mix of different cultures. Sri Lanka is especially famous for curries. These spicy stews are served with rice. In Sri Lanka, they are often made with fish. They can also be based on meat, lentils, or vegetables.

STREET FOOD

Many people buy fast food from street stalls. Kottu roti is a very popular dish. It uses leftover roti, a flatbread, cut into strips. The flatbread is mixed with vegetables, meat, and spices. Then everything is stir-fried. Hoppers are also popular. These are pancakes made from rice flour and coconut milk. They are cooked in a bowl shape. A fried egg is often cooked inside.

GODAMBA ROTI

These flatbreads are common in Sri Lanka. They can be served plain alongside a curry or wrapped around a savory filling.

Ingredients:
- 3 cups of flour
- 2–3 cups of vegetable oil
- salt for seasoning
- water

Instructions:

1. Put the flour, salt, and 3 tablespoons of oil in a large bowl and mix them together.
2. Add water, a little bit at a time, until you have a soft dough. If it is too wet, add more flour.
3. Knead the dough for about 10 minutes.
4. Divide the dough into balls, slightly larger than a golf ball.
5. Put the balls into a shallow dish and add oil until they are completely covered. Cover it with a dish towel and leave for at least 6 hours.
6. Take a ball from the oil and use your hands to stretch and flatten it into a thin pancake.
7. Ask an adult to help you heat a wok or large frying pan. Fry the roti for about 30 seconds on each side.
8. Repeat steps 6 and 7 with the rest of the balls.

CHAPTER FIVE

HOLIDAYS AND CELEBRATIONS

The calendar in Sri Lanka is packed with colorful festivals. Most are related to one of the island's religions. Sri Lankans celebrate the New Year in April. People get ready by cleaning and painting their homes. They buy new clothes.

During this holiday you hear the sound of firecrackers and drums. Families share special meals. They also exchange gifts. They give offerings to the gods. People gather in the streets to play games.

These sweet treats are popular at New Year celebrations.

Families often gather to watch the pongal cooking.

HARVEST FESTIVAL

In January, Tamils celebrate the rice harvest. This four-day festival is called Thai Pongal. It also celebrates the longer days that spring will bring. People cook a special dish called *pongal*. It is made of rice, milk, sugar, nuts, and raisins. If the cooking pot overflows, this is thought to bring good luck.

CELEBRATING BUDDHA

The festival of Vesak Poya takes place in May. It always starts on a full moon. Sinhalas celebrate the life of the Buddha. People visit the temple to **meditate**. There are parades with colorful lanterns.

Esala Perahera takes place in Kandy. A temple there is said to hold one of the Buddha's teeth. The festival honors this sacred tooth. It also honors Hindu gods. Thousands of people come to watch the parade. There are elephants dressed in colorful fabrics. One of them carries the tooth. There are acrobats, jugglers, dancers, and musicians.

FACT

Sri Lankans celebrate their independence from Britain each year on February 4. There are speeches and parades. People sing the national anthem as the flag is raised.

The Esala Perahera celebrations are full of color and music.

CHAPTER SIX

SPORTS AND RECREATION

Cricket is the most popular sport in Sri Lanka. This bat-and-ball game is played by teams of 11 players. Some matches last for several days! Many people also play **amateur** cricket. Crowds gather to watch professional matches. They are played around the island. The national team is one of the best in the world. They won the World Cup in 1996.

Many people think that Kumar Sangakkara was one of the best cricket players ever.

OTHER SPORTS

Volleyball is the official national sport of Sri Lanka. Many people play this game. They also play beach volleyball. This version is played on sand by teams of two. Sri Lankans also enjoy soccer, rugby, badminton, and netball.

KANAA ALLEEMA

This is a popular children's game. It is often played as part of the New Year celebrations by adults as well as children. You need a large group of people, a big open space, and a blindfold.

1. Use chalk or another method to mark out a large circle on the ground.
2. Choose one person to be "it" and blindfold them.
3. The person who is "it" must try to tag the other players.
4. Anyone who is tagged or runs outside the circle is out.
5. If the blindfolded person runs out of the circle, someone guides them back in.
6. The last person who hasn't been caught is the winner.

GLOSSARY

amateur (AM-uh-chur)
done for fun rather than as a job

Buddhism (BOO-diz-um)
a religion based on following the teachings of the man known as the Buddha

civil war (SIV-ul WAR)
a war fought between different groups within a country, rather than between different countries

fortress (FOR-tris)
a structure that is built to defend against attack

grassland (GRAS-land)
a large area of land with grasses but few trees

harbor (HAR-bur)
a body of water along a coast that provides a safe place for ships to dock

independent (in-de-PEN-dent)
not ruled over by anyone else

indigenous (in-DI-jen-us)
native to a place

meditate (MED-i-tayt)
to relax the mind and body by thinking quietly and deeply

rain forest (RANE FOR-ist)
a type of thick, dense forest that receives a lot of rain

temple (TEM-pul)
a sacred building where religious rituals take place

READ MORE

Marsico, Katie. *Buddhism*. North Mankato, MN: Cherry Lake Publishing, 2017.

O'Brien, Cynthia. *Cultural Traditions in Sri Lanka*. New York: Crabtree Publishing Company, 2017.

Sullivan, Laura L. *Sri Lanka*. New York: Cavendish Square, 2019.

INTERNET SITES

10 Fun Facts About Sri Lanka
multiculturalkidblogs.com/2018/03/23/fun-facts-sri-lanka/

Places to Visit in Sri Lanka
srilanka.travel

Sri Lanka: Introduction and Quick Facts
britannica.com/place/Sri-Lanka

INDEX

OTHER BOOKS IN THIS SERIES